Poems for Recycling Lives

Dr David H. Dighton

MEDICAUSE

Copyright © 2024

by David H. Dighton

All rights reserved.

No portion of this book may be reproduced in any form without written permission from the publisher or author, except as permitted by UK and U.S. copyright law.

About the Author

Dr. David H. Dighton qualified at the London Hospital Medical College in 1966 with MB and BS (London) degrees. In 1970, after a short time in NHS general practice, he became a British Heart Foundation Fellow in Cardiology at St. George's Hospital Hyde Park Corner, London, working with cardiologists Dr Aubrey Leatham and Dr Alan Harris. In 1973, he became a MRCP(UK), and later became a Lecturer (London University) in Medicine and Cardiology at Charing Cross Hospital, London.

In 1980, the Vrije University Hospital in Amsterdam appointed him as Chef de Clinique (Assistant Professor). Having returned to the UK in 1982, he worked both in his own private medical practice in Loughton, Essex (The Loughton Clinic, was initially established in 1973 as a medical nursing home), and at the Wellington Hospital, London. In 2000, he started a private diagnostic cardiac centre specialising in heart disease prevention and the early detection of heart and artery disease (The Cardiac Centre Loughton).

He retired from practice having been a medical student and doctor for 60 years, having experience birth, life and death from many angles; living alongside the lives of many thousands of patients from which have derived many poetic thoughts which hopefully might help others negotiate their lives.

Other Books by the Author

Eat to Your Heart's Content. The diet and lifestyle for a healthy h eart.(2003). HeartShield.
ISBN: 0-9551072-0-2

HeartSense. How to look after your heart.(2006). HeartShield.
ISBN: 0-9551072-1-0

The NHS: Our Sick Sacred Cow: Causes and Cures (2023)
ISBN: 978-1-3999-6027-4 (also an ebook).

How to Become Heart-Smart. A User's Guide to Heart Health and Heart Disease Prevention. (2023 1st Ed./2nd Ed. 2024. ISBN: 978-1-3999-7461-5 (also an ebook).

Who Loses Wins. Winning Weight Loss Battles: A 'Fat Mentality' v A 'Fit Mentality' (2024).
ISBN: 978-1-7385207-1-8 (ebook: 978-1-7385207-2-5)

Doctors, Nurses & Patients. How to Survive Medical Practice. (2024)
ISBN: 978-1-7385207-5-6 (also an ebook, ISBN: 978-1-7385207-6-3)

The Art and Science of Medical Practice (2024)
ISBN: 9781738520770 (hardback); 9781738520732 (Paperback); 9781738520749 (e-book)

e-books from https://stan.store/drdhd001001

In Preparation:
Essential Cardiology for Students.

CONTACT

For more information, go to 'www.daviddighton.com' or email: david@daviddighton.com or daviddighton@loughtonclinic.org

POEMS FOR RECYCLING LIVES

Contents

Detailed Contents	XII
Preface	1
1. Senryu for Life, Biases & Relationships	5
2. Poetic Thoughts of Love, Life & Loss	30
Index	125

Detailed Contents

Senryu

Senryu on Biases

The Halo Bias, p9
The Framing Bias, p9
Paradoulia, p10
Statistical Bias, p10
Hindsight Bias, p10
Hot Hand Bias, p11
Inamorata Bias, p11

The Greener Grass Bias, p12
Zeigarnik Bias, p12
Zero Sum Bias, p13
Ambiguity Bias, p13
Fun Bias, p14
Geography Bias, p14
Overload Bias, p15
Intervention Bias, p15

Relationships: How they Function

On Affection, p16 – 17
On Control, p18
On Inclusion, p19

About Relationships

At the End, p20
The Gift of Love, p21
No Return to Sender, p21
Couples Discovered, p22

Love Defined, p22 – p23
A Place for Art: Life, p24 – p27
Overload Bias, p28
Intervention Bias, p28
Medical Senryu, p29

Poetic Thoughts

Wasted Dreams, p31 – p32
You Ask me Why, p33
Escape: Your True Self Waiting, p34 – p36
True Love Waits, p37
Where Will We Be? p38
Success, p39
Eyes, p40 – p41
Unrequited, p42
Steps, p43 – p44
Soul, p45 – p46
Selfless Teaching, p47
Re-Birth, p48 – p49
Pour Love into Your Words, p50 – p51
Try Resisting, p52 – p53
Cup of Love, p54 – p55
Validated Valentine, p56 – p57
No Use Without You, p58 – p59

The Good Doctor & The Art of Medicine, p60 -p61
Experienced Words, p62
Love and Honour, p63
Seasonal Embrace, p64 – p66
Soul, p67 – p68
Spirituality, p69 – p71
Steps, p72 – p73
Being Blessed, p74 – p75
The Wind. p76
Coincidence, p77 – p78
I know Your Are There, p79
Millennium Prayer, p80 – p81
One Last Prayer, p82 – p83
Sapphire Sea, p84
Search for a Better You, p85
Seeing Forever, p86 – p87
Ancestors, p88
Heaven and Earth, p88
'Feeling Bad', p89
Trust Me, p90 – p91

Fool if You Think I Love You, p92 – p93

A Busy Life, p94

Love at Peace, p95 – p96

Rejection, 97 – p99

Surrender, p100 – p101

Doors of Destiny, p102

Ready to Return, p103 – p104

Ideas, p105 – p107

Airport Bustle, p108 – p109

The Cold Hand of Indifference, p110

Time Passes, p111

Invisa Homines, p112 – p113

Peace or Progress, p114

Judgement Day, 115 – p116

Laundry, p117

Peace, p118

Black and White Snapshot, p119 – p120

Trust, p121 – p122

Unite, p123 – p124

Preface

Some seventeen syllable, non-classical poetic forms of Haiku are called Senryu. Unlike the prescribed form of Haiku, I have not kept to the 5-7-5, three-line form; they are also not seasonal or about nature. I see mine merely as disciplined exercises, expressing ideas in the most succinct form possible. Few of my poetic thoughts are rhyming; I see them as forms of poetic expression, the subjects of which are life and its judgement biases, loss and love.

My writing has roots in scientific writing, every word being chosen for a specific purpose, but here aiming to colour meaning with individually interpretable, poetic expression; sensitive illusion in contrast to formulaic scientific specificity.

I have attempted to go where poetic content lives: beyond the peaks of exact meaning, through the valleys of essence and personal interpretation, into the realms of the spiritual: all-accepting, non-judgmental frames of mind that so many have too little time for. From what other aspect of consciousness can one express feelings of love, beauty, stress and loss, all of which lack explicit definitions, but all of which have their serious individual meaning?

In any collection of thoughts like this, there will be only a few that will resonate for each person. Our search for appropriate knowledge and direction is always a similar quest. My aim is for each reader to find at least one item they regard as a gem; one that speaks to them and enables a better understanding and extra insight into life.

Chapter One

Senryu for Life,

Biases & Relationships

川柳

Short,
Seventeen syllable,
Crystallised thoughts,
To clarify life.

As we ponder,
Thinking slow,
All our conclusions
Are tainted by bias.

Senryu on Bias

Thoughts
Drawn through our channels
Of belief and value,
All emerge biased.

Our Assumptions,
Like a prison door,
Can shut out,
The light of wisdom.

The Halo Bias

Smitten by
Charisma and prescience,
Judgement is
Blinded by awe.

The Framing Bias

Bodies are more
Tempting dressed;
Data more believable
Well displayed

Paradoulia

Man on the moon;
Jesus in the shroud:
Imagination makes
faces.

Statistical Bias

Can a mean represent
My difference
from them all,
And what I am?

Hindsight Bias

Hindsight is all we have
To help foresight,
But lacks perfection.

Hot Hand Bias

With luck smiling
How can chance
Not favour me
As a prescient being?

After many defeats
Success seems unlikely
And action stunted.

Inamorata Bias

Love accepted
Confirms an angel;
A love scorned,
Connotes emptiness.

The Greener Grass Bias

With contentment,
life is apt.
With discontent the unknown
Looms brighter.

Zeigarnik Bias

What fascinates most
Is not the complete,
But often
The incomplete.

Zero Sum Bias

If life losses are minus
And gains plus:
Can their sum
Add to zero?

Ambiguity Bias

Find the definite.
Ignore the indefinite:
Embrace ambiguity.

Fun Bias

Without having fun,
Despite all other
Fulfilment,
Is life just work?

Geography Bias

Is here better;
Or is it there?
If we move,
Will it be what we want?

If here is good,
And there is unknown,
Why might there,
Be better than here?

Overload Bias

Is doing more,
Our life's secret?
Can our doing less,
Be the answer?

Intervention bias

Undecided?
Is action better
Than no action,
Or the reverse?

Relationships:
How They Function

On Affection

Ripples through silk;
Faces through glass.
Care through love,
Death through separation.

So many want love;
Need loving:
Waste it not
On those disinterested

Waste no love,
On those unwilling,
Or disinclined
To receive it.

Never expect love
From those unable
Or disinclined to
Give it.

Imagination comes easy;
Relationships require
Some endeavour

At the start of love
There is longing,
In the end
There's always regret.

On Control

Control only
To help those unable;
Use it to direct
Those lost.

Be controlled
Only by the capable,
When in need
Of direction.

On Inclusion

Enjoy the same interests
As partners;
Respect any
Differences.

Never impose
Your interests
On others without
Enthusiasm.

Seek those
Who share your purpose,
Not those who will only
Foster their own.

About Relationships

At The End

Let them go;
Let it hurt;
Let it heal;
Open your heart,
Only to love.

Believe in
Truth of feelings.
Cherish only those who
Will value you.

The Gift of Love

Each gift of true love,
Comes wrapped:
In unique tones,
For those intended.

No Return to Sender

The gift of love
Once given,
May seem rejected,
But seldom withdrawn.

Couples Discovered

Both loving
And liking,
Can together define
A lasting couple.

Love Defined

Self and ego
Must both resign
And submit,
Before love
Can be found.

Without affection
And no control,
Life will be
One of servitude.

Relationships start
Well-meaning,
And so often end
In oppression.

A mutual sense of beauty
Attracts us;
Then mutual needs
Disrupt us.

A Place for Art

Life

Surround yourself
With beauty.
Learn eternal values
Not worldly costs.

Every life
Has context and purpose:
And a background
Of your art.

Every life needs
Context and purpose;
Hoping for love
And fulfilment.

Wherever we roam;
And with whom,
We must return,
Alone to ourselves.

Activity consumes life;
Forms memories
Denies actuality

Activity on hold,
Exposes us to solitude
And our self.

Recording life
Photo by photo
Relegates life
To history.

Recording life
Photo by photo
Relegates life
To reliving.

Aspire to
Succinctness and
Clarity:
They will combat confusion.

In the beginning,
Understanding.
Then words;
Then more comprehension.

All'inizio,
comprensione.
Poi parole.
Poi più comprensione.

В начале,
Понимание.
Потом слова.
Потом больше.

Au début,
La compréhension.
Puis les mots.
Puis plus compréhension.

Στην αρχή
κατανόηση.
Μετά λέξεις.
Μετά κατανόηση.

Overload Bias

Is doing more,
Our life's secret?
Or might doing less,
Be the answer?

Intervention Bias

Undecided?
Is action better
Than no action,
Or the reverse?

Medical Senryu

Prevention is so much
Better than cure,
Because cure,
Is indeed rare.

Lacking knowledge,
You could die,
While worrying about
All the wrong things.

Ask those who claim
To know nothing
If their experience
Connotes more.

Chapter Two

Poetic Thoughts of Love, Life & Loss

Wasted Dreams?

With you in my dreams,
I found just how much love,
I had within.

With you in my dreams,
I found my true heart,
And what it might mean.

With you in my dreams,
I found my destiny,
And someone to fill its empty halls.

With you in my dreams,
I had to confront myself:
All that I am; all that I was; all that I
am not; all I could be.

With you in my dreams,
I never once dreamed,
Of missing you.

With you in my dreams,
I had to learn that dreams,
Alas,
Are little else.

You Ask Me Why

You ask me why,
I don't look into your eyes?
In my eyes you might see uncertainty;
My needs;
My hopes;
My secrets,
My vulnerability.

In your eyes I might see
Cool indifference:
Freedom not to love.
Your doubt;
Your insecurity;
Nothing to call mine.

Escape:
Your True Self Lies Waiting

Your true self lies waiting:
Waiting to emerge from childhood,
With its lack of inhibitions:
Slipping on the shoe of adulthood.

Your true self lies waiting:
Wanting no puppetry,
Strings, pulled by others,
If cut . . . released to be yourself.

Your true self lies waiting:
Waiting to drift,
To float free on love and caring;
Faith, trust, and respect, insuring
safety.

Your true self lies waiting:
Waiting to escape any control,
That pain can hide,
Denying you the right to love.

Your true self lies waiting:
To travel where destiny dictates,
As chance may find,
Safety in the arms of love.

Safe.
So safe;
So very safe.
To love without condition . . . you'll see!

Trusting.
So trusting;
So very trusting.
To love without fear . . . you'll see!

Your true self lies waiting:
Waiting for a purpose.
A commitment,
Awaiting a status.

Your true self lies waiting:
Waiting for real strength;
For worthiness in grace:
Happy to give love;
Happy to take love;
Happy to make love.

True Love Waits

Only true love,
Recognises the need to go away,
And the need to return.

Only true love,
Has the time to wait . . . regardless,
As other feelings fade.

Where Will We Be?

Who knows where our atoms will be,
Yours and mine?
Seen in the future,
Only through the windows of a black
hole?

How many souls now rest in stars:
In Orion,
The Milky Way?
Or other Universes,
Not ours to see.
Not ours to know.

So quiet —
Let us be.

Success

Every disappointment,
Is a liberation;
Every success,
An imprisonment.

Who will be my inspiration,
My need,
My need to be,
My motivation?

What may not seem possible now,
Was once then.
What once seemed necessary,
Became a life.

Eyes

Can eyes,
Steal love's vision,
Hiding it where,
Emotions form and fold?

Can eyes,
Look . . .
With knowing or indifference,
To feelings young and old?

Can eyes
Deny a harmony it's tune,
By playing notes,
In keys untold?

Enough to ask . . . and time to tell:
Eyes,
Hold their fix-ed gaze,
On those they love,
And those they must behold.

Unrequited

Love, unreturned,
Unsatisfied; dissatisfied:
Only ever,
One half of two,
One lonely singleton.

Waste no further time.
Look forward,
Never back.
What our mind knows,
Our heart may not be ready
To confirm.

Steps

Be thankful,
Not only for your path,
But for each journey;
For the experiences of each day,
And every step within it.

We all have a path,
With each step our own;
Even when accompanied.

Each step our own creation:
Willing, unwilling;
Mercurial or leaden.
Our destination only imagined,
Never truly seen,
Except by chance.

How can we guess our end,
Being sure,
Only of each step we take?
Past and future steps,
Awaiting their release from illusion.

Soul

We are born, our soul
Unscathed,
Despite the commands of ego,
Needing its uniqueness
Recognised.

Cloaked by fear of pain,
We must protect,
Bury,
And fool our soul,
From what life intends.

If we should find realisation,
We will have undone,
Uncovered,
Or rediscovered,
The mantle of our civilisation;

That wrapped us with
Indoctrination,
Manufactured by education, learning
and training,
Never to return to our
Foetal psycho-virginity,
To our *Tabula rasa.*

Now our real soul floats in a dynamic
universe;
With our past,
And purpose,
Complete in one objective:
To die free of chains

Selfless Teaching

The noblest of teaching,
Comes only from the dead;
Where beyond all need
For recognition,
They selflessly bring us wisdom.

Re-Birth

Escape to where nothing binds;
Where ties dissolve, no longer ours.
Without pride, guilt or resentment.
No wishes, wants or reactions.
No demands.
Content with everything;
Content with nothing;
Aware of everything;
Knowing nothing.

Fulfilled by noise,
And the music of silence;
With us;
But not of us.
Born alone to die alone;
To live alone,
Save for those,
With another destiny.

Our only state of grace;
Closest to the unborn,
Closest to those now dead;
But ready for the rebirth,
Borne by love.

Pour Love Into Words

Pour love into words,
And devotion into deeds.
Fear no loss,
Since nothing lasts.

Fear not love's passing,
For even fleeting love enriches.
No love is ever lost;
No love ever wasted.

While our ego plans its path,
Remember one certainty:
What is now.
So keep only one closed eye,
And pencil in the future.

Kneed sincerity into every thought,
And honesty into every feeling.
Spurn anger, criticism, and cynical views,
For these can induce destruction.

See only love in all you view.
Make love,
The only point:
And find peace.

And from that serenity,
Our soul can view its goal:
Loving grace:
In perpetuum.

Now free of selfish ego,
Open that one closed eye,
And see with both eyes,
Love fit only for forever.

Try Resisting

One cannot fight it;
One cannot plan it;
One cannot resist it;
It's force overwhelms.

One cannot deny it;
Work with it;
Or against it;
It is devouring.

You will know its touch;
Know its glance;
Its dreams inescapable,
In desperation.

It can absorb us;
Control us;
Its longing;
Making us absent.

Addicting;
Obsessing;
Laughing;
Tormenting;
Crying;
Absorbing;
Fulfilling;
Depersonalising,
Wrenching love.

Cup of Love

Take only those,
Who by their presence,
Fill your cup with love.

Avoid all,
Who would drink their fill,
From unreciprocated generosity.

What welcome need,
Can bring,
A genuine smile
From a gifted soul:
Flagging kindliness
From deep within.

Others can make a similar face,
But a sardonic smile,
Betraying detachment,
With smiling malevolence.

Smiles betray
What lies within:
Where interest lies,
Come eyes fixed parallel -
To hearts engaged.

When disinterest reigns -
The face reveals,
What cannot be denied.

Validated Valentine

Can love and beauty speak?
With soft glances, so tardy in their parting?
With one touch that leaves it dew life-long?
With kisses sparking lifelong glow?
With closeness, grasped in love's arms,
Once fleeting lust is spent?

What thought. What feeling,
Infuses beauty's dream?
That selfless care which only lovers know?
That honesty which knows regret?
Faithfulness, which pride does make?

Or, loves devotion which fruits in
Spring,
And ripens slow to Autumn"s close?

Yes, all of these, which in the grasp of
night,
And the flights of day,
Recharge my love.

No Use Without You

I am no use without you,
So desiccate me,
And sprinkle me on
Christmas pudding.

I am no use without you,
So fashion me into a close fit garment,
To clutch me close on
Christmas Day.

I am no use without you,
So liquidise me,
And drink me mulled with wine.

I am no use without you,
So weave me into silk pants,
And wear me intimate and firm.

I am no use without you,
So chop and fry me,
And enjoy me for breakfast.

I am no use without you,
So pulp me into lipstick,
And wear me for each betraying kiss.

I am no use without you,
So make me into your sun and stars,
To light your separate life.

The Good Doctor
&
The Art of Medicine

Who will hold a troubled hand,
And take guardianship,
Of enough hope and trust,
To settle a troubled mind?

Who will step forth with knowledge enough,
Sufficient to make disease submit;
Halting its progress,
Against the odds?

Who will come forth with fortitude enough,
To assume the care of a life, or a death,
And through trust and confidence,
Encourage a smile to break the grip of fear, pain, and grief?

Who will come forth,
With humility enough,
To step beyond the science,
And embrace the human spirit?

Only those who can become
Complete physicians.

Experienced Words

Experienced words,
From older tongues,
Fly ad nauseam,
Into novices' ears;
Although heard,
Not always heeded.

From the events that diminish us,
With fear and resentment;
To those that enliven us,
Evoking our fascination
and self-esteem,
Knowledge assumes more usefulness,
Once marinated in experience.

Love and Honour

Honour is to love,
As love is to honour.
Love sooner lost,
Is honour sooner gained.

When life,
Tangled in the thorns of conflict,
Bloods the thighs
Of anguished lovers.
Pain, borne of parting,
Washed in tears,
A wanting mist,
Condensing on shields of honour.

Then, silence;
Except for recurring
Drum-beat memories.
Revived only in dreams.

Seasonal Embrace

Cold in a white,
Loveless mist of winter,
Dead branches extend,
Towards hope:
Searching for warmth:
Waiting for care,
And the touch of concern.
Awaiting colour,
From flowers,
And offspring's seeds;
Hope and happiness enshrined.

Then, embracing kindness,
A shining sun,
Smiles in recognition;
Pumping green into black;
Sweetening decay;
Giving way to life,
And leaves of friendship:
Sprouting and touching;
Caressing,
In speechless intimacy:
Thence to grow,
Or soon to die:
Worthless, forgotten,
Or remembered.

Then Spring;
Its buds of love,
Stuck with joyous resin:
Bursts euphoric,
Emboldened with entwinement.
Unfolding,
As wet as any morning passion:
Kissing the day,
Glorious with excitement;
Ready to bask in mutual nurture,
Folding exhausted,
Awaiting terse 'Good-bye's',
And gazing sighs,
Too long in parting shadows.

Soul

We are born with a soul,
Unscathed,
Commanded by an ego,
With uniqueness,
Forming.

Cloaked in fear of pain,
We must protect,
Bury,
And fool,
Our soul from what life,
Will make of us.

Then, if by chance,
We find realisation,
By undoing, uncovering
and rediscovering
Our true selves:

Having thrown off some mantles of
Civilisation;
Divesting ourselves of
That stealthy indoctrination,
A shroud made of assumption,
Education,
And rational thought.

Might we return to our foetal
Psycho-virginity,
With madness or dementia,
To find our soul intact;
Its past and purpose,
Complete with life's objective?
Dying as free from life's clutter,
As when our eyes first opened.

Spirituality

Through the doors of boundless fact,
Lies spirituality.
Selflessly inspired,
By love,
Aeons awaited,
As slowly,
We step towards eternity.

Never seen or heard,
Only by sensibility,
Is it known,
Its essence barely perceived;
And so easily ignored,
As faces,
Words and actions,
Obfuscate our view.

You will know it,
From shoulders that never tire.
You will know it,
Because it knows our soul.
You will know it,
Because its attention never wanes;
Because it bears no secret,
Bringing only inspiration.

Know it,
As selfless energy,
Know it,
As its finger points to God.
Know it,
Because it procures at-one-ness.
Know it,
Because its boundless spirit
Feeds our growth.
Know it,
From its unconditional,
Boundless energy,

On offer:
That state of grace,
Allowing a glimpse Heaven.

Steps

Be thankful,
Not only for your path ,
But for each journey:
Experiences of every day,
And for each step .

We all have our path,
Heading beside others.
Each step our own,
Each our own creation,
Be it willing or unwilling;
Mercurial or leaden.
Our final destination,
Can only be imagined;
Never foreseen,
Except by chance.

We only know for sure,
Each thought and step we take.
Is all else illusion?

Being Blessed

She told me I was blessed.
She told me of the angel
On my shoulder.
Yet with self-effacing humility,
Of no other I have met,
She knew not this angel's name:
Yet I was soon to know -
My mother's name was Florence.

My only hope: she left me,
Freed of all anxiety for my welfare,
Able to stand alone with all she left
me:

A mountain of composure,
And security,
Built from the love of an angel.
A gift, no man can make,
For it was given of perfect
Motherhood.

As friends might become lovers,
And acquaintances friends,
We change state,
Mind unchanged.
What we behold sees change,
Yet, as it ever was.

Truly blessed.
There is no higher state of being,
No self-esteem,
Greater to be cherished,
Than being worthy
Of an angel's love.

The Wind

Where would your judgement be,
Floating in the clouds;
When the last shreds of discord,
Seep away?

It doesn't matter:
The treading drone of lorries,
The harmony of wind splayed grass:
Offering symphonic accompaniment,
To meditation.

We feel distinct,
No more than the wind,
Or the foaming sea,
Or the ox and cart,
And mother nature.

Coincidence

There is no chance;
Only coincidence.
There is no need,
But necessity.

You were not with me just because
You wanted to be.
I was not with you just because I
Wanted to be.
We belonged.

What choice did I have, but to love
you?
I was overcome by your presence;
By your beauty,
By your modesty,

By your benevolence.
Overcome by mutual understanding;
By your uncharted worth.
Overcome by your happiness;
An easy synchrony of embarrassed laughter.

I Know You are There

A landscape surrounds me,
Placing my existence,
Under sky, mountains, sea, and storm.
I can close my eyes,
I know my place.

Like your presence surrounding me:
Pervading my life;
I need not touch you,
Need not see you.
I know you are there,

Like the grass beneath my feet,
Like the air I breath,
Like the sun on my face,
Warm with radiance,
I can always feel your presence.

Millennium Prayer

Nothing can be built,
Without a past;
And nothing achieved,
Without a future.

Reject impatience,
Replace it with serenity.
Let peace becalm you,
And let the joy of life immerse you.

No flame burns brighter,
Under an insistent stare;
No flower
More quickly blossoms,
By any plea you dare.

In this you can trust:
Your destiny has its path,
A place; a time,
And nothing wasted.

Tread higher,
Only on steps of experience.
Even though we slip and fall,
Mistakes can guide us.

What has been,
And what will be,
Both exist,
Because they must.

Is this what true love sees;
What true love hears?
Is this what true love feels,
Once found?

One Last Prayer

May your heart welcome peace as no stranger;
With happiness and laughter
in all your days.
May the love you have received,
Forever light your way,
And the love you have to give,
Never diminished.
May providence free your hurt and pain,
And afford you freedom
To love again.

Let Fortune shine upon you,
And bring you more to give.
May justice lead you to mercy.
And faith to forgiveness.
Come to realise:
We are worthy only of the
love we bestow.

A Sapphire Sea

Six diamond stars,
Might guide your heart,
Across a sapphire sea,
Where love awaits,
To perform its part,
For mutual love and destiny.

Search for a Better You

Your search to find a better you,
Must open first your heart:
To find that love and giving free,
That are your better part.

Don't look too far, or look too deep,
God's blessings are a given.
On them you must feed,
Whether great, small or driven.

Seeing Forever

Pour love into your words,
And devotion into your deeds.
Fear no loss,
For nothing lasts.

Fear not love's passing,
For even fleeting love survives:
No love is ever lost:
It lives on in other lives.

While your ego plans its path,
Remember only this:
Existence . . . is for now alone.
With no forever bliss.

Kneed sincerity into every thought,
And honesty into every feeling.
Spurn anger, criticism,
And cynical views:
They lead to destruction.

View love in all you see;
And make love,
The only point:
If peace you seek.

From serenity,
Let your soul view its goal:
Loving grace,
In perpetuum.

Now free of selfish ego,
Open that one closed eye,
And with both eyes,
Glimpse love everlasting.

Ancestors

As we live,
Through the lives of our ancestors.
Our ancestors,
Live through us.

Heaven & Earth

When you think you've been given
Heaven,
It may be Hell.
When you think you've been given
the Earth,
Take it, and don't rebel!

'Feeling Bad'

How much love is wasted,
On those vain and vacuous souls,
Whose only claim upon it,
Is their hair that falls in rolls?

How much love is wasted,
On those with a beautiful face,
Whose true heart and inner worth,
Is no more than wasted space?

Trust Me

When somebody says:
"You can trust me!".
Or: "My honour is not in doubt."
Suspect that they are simply lying,
And no more than a lustful lout.

If they say they'll love you forever,
If they say they'll always be true,
Suspect it's your body they're after,
For both men and women . . .
nothing new!

If someone says they love you,
From the bottom of their heart,
Run, or stay for ever:
It's the end, or just the start.

Fool if You Think I Love You!

If the one you love ever says:
"Don't get the wrong idea",
They have in mind,
You're trying in vain to get near.

If the times they want to see you,
Are not often, and apart.
That someone you think is special,
Is attached to another heart.

If they avoid tender kisses;
And don't want to hold you tight.
That someone you think is special,
Is thinking of nothing but flight.

You can't make any person,
Adore and love you true.
So if you want to make a real fool of yourself,
Love someone, who doesn't love you.

A Busy Life

Your friends are close beside you,
They fill your every day,
They need to feel needed,
At work, at home and play.

That leaves me feeling lonely,
Outside your busy life,
So where does that leave me,
Within your, Oh, so busy strife?
Once a lover and best friend,
Now neither friend or wife.

Love at Peace

All that is left,
Of tear-tinged reminiscence;
Is the ambivalence of lonely freedom:
The stillness of solitude;
A vacant sense of loss;
The certainty of uncertainty.

The odyssey we need,
Must find another trail,
Replacing all,
We took for granted.

True love at peace:
From a unique match,
Seemingly gone forever,
Is never lost,
But on angel's wings,
Flies back to heaven.

In no more conflict;
In no more pain.
We are ordained,
A sacred chalice,
Half-filled with adoration,
Awaiting another donation.

Rejection

Floating in elegance,
Fit for Spring.
A joy to roving eyes,
And yearning lips:
Alas, not mine.

In times past,
On a distant beach;
In a quiet forest,
Tender kisses once were mine.

Though I create,
One thousand petalled pillows,
Would I earn a credit?
If I travelled to the far reaches of
time,

Would I be thought too silly;
To love and to kiss?

If I wrote endless poetry,
Exposing my virtues and weaknesses,
Would I be thought too clever?

Call 'Halt!'.
Transfer your love;
As an early goodnight,
Marks the last rejection,
With a peck on your cheek!

Go!
Nothing,
Even doing nothing,
Will get you closer,
To an unfeeling heart.

Don't watch;
Don't waste your time,
As lesser suitors satisfy their needs,
And without trying,
Steal your desires.

Surrender

When companionship is sufficient,
But not enough:
Enwrap yourself with tenderness,
Borne of trust.
Entwine yourself with selfless
Affection,
Conceived unquestioned.
Surrender your body to a power,
Charmed by the arrest,
Of conscious space and time.

When friendship is precious,
But not enough:
Step unashamed,
Into the spotlight of your being.

Surrender your passion,
To one who desires rapture.
Surrender your guilt,
To one who desires absolution,
Through ecstasy,
To conviction:
Knowing that every such moment,
Enriches our soul.

Doors of Destiny

The house of destiny,
Has many doors,
Some open, some blocked,
Some locked,
To other worlds.

Walk through,
To suffer one destiny.
Walk not,
To suffer another.

Ready to Return

Ready for my return,
Having reached journey's end;
Through conflict and challenge,
Back to your love and teaching.

You taught me what I was,
And where my values lay,
By sharing them,
And anointing me with peace.

You sent me forth to test my values,
Knowing that I would suffer:
Knowing I would find no value;
And the futility of searching.

So now it's time.
To await your grace,
And togetherness.

Ideas

So often born to flounder,
On the rocks of practicality,
Ideas can lie squandered,
Spirit broken,
Waiting for another time.

Only one person,
Needs perception enough,
To know their merit.
Great ideas,
Appealing through simplicity,
Answer many questions,
And profit all inspired,

Big ideas,
Conceived beyond the hope
Of others,
Can bring the owner tolerant
ridicule,
Risking the scorn of error.
Carried forward with energy and
commitment,
Can lead to success,

Good ideas,
While common,
May lack the time,
In one lifetime,
To make them live,
And offer fortune,

Small ideas,
May have their moment,
But like the morning mist,
Can be dismissed,
By greater minds.

Airport Bustle

A bustling clog of humanity;
Dressed for comfort,
In tones of mass-production.
Older men straining over
Tight trousers.
Vacant stares fit for solitude.
Children sleeping,
Children screaming,
Wreaking havoc.
Unfamiliar parents,
With no escape!
Their wish to be back at work,
Bringing misery to all.

Telephones pressed to faces,
Assuaging boredom.
Twittering verbiage,
Distracting tension.
Baseball caps anticipating sunshine;
Thin and tired smiles,
Fearing anxiety.
Fearing flying?
Fearing death?
First pint - 6am!

Bags worn, bags carried, bags trailed:
Can't waste time,
Getting to where we want to waste time,
As cabin-luggage-luggers,
Save ten minutes at a distant carousel!

The Cold Hand of Indifference

Hold their hand,
If you dare.
And let them flow,
Through innate senses:
The Love;
The Fear;
The Cunning;
The Lust;
Or feigned interest.

Beware of words,
That fail to match,
The cold hand of indifference!

Time Passes

In this moment,
And only now,
Am I alive.

There are no yesterdays to relive;
Just to be remembered.

No tomorrows yet to live,
Only those expected.

Some hoping,
They are now.

And, as if at once,
Through wasted existence,
Tomorrow flows fast,
And soon becomes then.

Invisa Homines

Rising bloated
Through the treacle of vanity;
Through acid ego
And sanctimonious pride,
They come:
The odious.

Seeking power,
More attention.
Displacing modesty,
Displacing the unempowered;
Displacing the benign;
Displacing friends and families,
Happy to extend their succour,
To notional enemies —
To homogenous crowds,

Indistinguishable when naked;
Trying to live a virtuous,
Bypassed life.
Hoping only for peace,
For happy powerlessness;
As are the easily ignored.

Peace or Progress?

Build a bridge
And visit mother in a day!
Now build a better bridge:
And visit mother in half a day.
Now an even better bridge:
And visit her in 3 hours!
Now with the best bridge:
One can't decide
Whether to visit her at all.

Progress absorbs one mind,
But weakens another.
Progress can gladden one heart,
But sadden another.
The game of progress is a pastime.
Aimed at finding,
Love and peace.

Judgement Day

Is it love or just plain lust?
Is (s)he good, or is (s)he bad?
Is (s)he simply the best,
Or simply the worst?
Is (s)he false, or is (s)he true?
A villain, or a Knight?
A saviour or destroyer?
Trustworthy — or full of lies?
Be (s)he right, yet ugly,
Or handsome, and wrong?
A love to give up life for,
Or to forsake?

Decide, and be damned
Or decide and be blessed:
Decide you must,
At fate's behest.
For here it is, and here alone,
Where Titans of impulse and good sense clash,
Destiny is born.

Within the balance of
Luck-lustered judgement.
Hope for Solomon's eye,
To see,
As clear as ever it can be,
Which turn to take,
And for your future,
Nothing but a sweet life make.

Laundry

New love,
Hangs clean and wet;
Ready to crease and dry:
Like laundry.

Simple impressions form,
Draped over a line of respect;
Hanging limp,
Between the pillars:
Of fantasy and prospect.
Ready, without de-wrinkling
Experience,
To swaddle us in rapture.

Peace

Peace rests lonely;
Grown from seed,
That thrives or dies,
In loving nurture,
Born of nature.

No other peace lies beyond,
Save as fleeting illusion:
In the optimistic lulls,
Between pessimistic storms,
To which all life must surrender.

Black and White Snapshot

The shutter opens - - -
With one millisecond of certainty - - -
And imprints us.

That's all I have of you:
Dis-animated.
De-personalised;
Your true self,
Hidden behind a conscious pose,
Cloaked in black anonymity,
On a white screen of expectancy.

Your beauty unmarked,
By the peace of print;
Unlined by intimacy.
Unruffled by fears,
Unstained by tears.

Self-colours suppressed,
In frozen monochrome.

Denied all expression.
Awaiting the motive warmth of a hand.
The painting of red on grey,
Pink on white,
Giving truth and life,
Back to captured reality.

Trust

Don't trust me with your body:
I might ravish it with tenderness.
Don't trust me with your mind:
I might strip it of uncertainty.

Don't trust me with your 'self':
I might unite with you.
Don't trust me with your joy:
You might never want for more.

Don't serve me your trust:
You might find honour.
Don't trust me with your fears:
You might find true peace.

Don't trust me with your secrets:
You might find friendship.
Don't trust me with your inner thoughts:
You might find understanding.

Don't trust me with your Commitment:
You might no longer feel lost.
Don't trust me with your kisses:
You might lose your heart.

Don't trust me with your self-esteem:
You might find dignity.
Don't trust me with your affection:
You might come to say: "I love you."

Unite

One look,
Can unite two hearts,
Anxious for love in the afternoon.

One telephone call,
Can unite two minds,
Each, thinking of the other.

Once two souls touch.
No words,
Need verify love.

When two spirits unite,
No hand,
Needs to manage
Love's purpose.

Index

A

absolution, 101
acquaintances, 75
addicting, 53
adulthood, 34
aeons, 69
ambiguity, 13
ancestors, 88
angel, 11, 74, 75, 95

anguished, 63
anonymity, 119
art, 24, 60
assumption, 68
assumptions, 8
atoms, 38
attention, 70, 112
autumn, 57
awe, 9

B

beach, 97
beautiful, 89
beauty, 2, 23, 24, 56, 77
beginning, 26
belief, 8
believable, 9
believe, 20
benevolence, 78
betray, 55

bias, 5, 8, 9, 10, 11, 12, 13, 14, 15, 28
biased, 8
black hole, 38
blessed, 74, 75, 116
blessings, 85
bliss, 86
boredom, 109
born, 45, 67, 105, 116
brighter, 12, 80
broken, 105

C

capable, 18
certainty, 50, 95, 119
chains, 46
chalice, 96
chance, 11, 35, 43, 67, 72, 77
charisma, 9
cherished, 75
Christmas pudding, 58

civilisation, 45
civilisation, 68
clarity, 26
coincidence, 77
colour, 2, 64
combat, 26
commitment, 36, 106, 122
companionship, 100
composure, 75
comprehension, 26
conflict, 63, 96, 103
confront, 31
consciousness, 2
contentment, 12
context, 24
control, 18, 53
conviction, 101
couple, 22
creation, 43, 72
criticism, 51, 87
crowds, 112
crying, 53

cunning, 110
cup, 54

D

dead, 47, 49
decay, 65
definite, 13
dementia, 68
deny, 52
denying, 35
de-personalised, 119
desperation, 52
destiny, 31, 35, 48, 81, 84, 102
destruction, 51, 87
devotion, 50, 57, 86
difference, 10
dignity, 122
direction, 3, 18
dis-animated, 119
discord, 76
disinclined, 16, 17

disinterested, 16, 55
dissatisfied, 42
doubt, 33, 90
dreams, 31, 32, 52, 63

E

ecstasy, 101
education, 46
ego, 22, 45, 50, 51, 67, 86, 87, 112
elegance, 97
embarrassed, 78
emotions, 40
emptiness, 11
endeavour, 17
endless, 98
energy, 70, 106
enthusiasm, 19
error, 106
escape, 35, 108
eternal, 24
excitement, 66

existence, 86
expectancy, 119
experience, 29, 62, 81, 117
eyes, 33, 40, 51, 55, 68, 79, 87, 97

F

faces, 16
faith, 34
families, 112
fantasy, 117
far reaches of time, 97
fascinates, 12
fascination, 62
fear, 36, 45, 61, 62, 67
feelings, 2, 20, 37, 40
flight, 92
flying, 109
fool, 45, 67, 93
foresight, 10
forgiveness, 83
fortitude, 61

fortune, 83
foster, 19
freedom, 82, 95
friends, 75, 94, 112
friendship, 65, 100, 122
fulfilment, 25
fulfilment, 14
fun, 14
future, 38, 44, 50, 80, 116

G

gaze, 41
generosity, 54
gift, 21, 75
glances, 56
glow, 56
God, 70, 85
grace, 36, 49, 51, 71, 87, 104
growth, 70
guilt, 48, 101

H

Haiku, 1
happiness, 64, 78, 82
harmony, 40, 76
heal, 20
heart, 20, 31, 42, 82, 84, 85, 89, 91, 92, 99, 114, 122
heaven, 95
heaven, 71, 88
hell, 88
hindsight, 10
home, 94
honour, 63, 90, 121
honour, 63
hoping, 25, 113
humanity, 108
humility, 61, 74
hurt, 20, 82

I

ideas, 1, 105, 106, 107
illusion, 2, 44, 73, 118
Imagination, 10, 17
imagined, 43, 72
imprisonment, 39
In perpetuum, 51, 87
inclusion, 19
incomplete, 12
indefinite, 13
indifference, 33, 40, 110
indoctrination, 68
inhibitions, 34
innate senses, 110
insecurity, 33
insight, 3
inspiration, 39, 70
interests, 19
interpretation, 2
Intervention, 15, 28
intimacy, 65, 119

intimate, 58

J

journey, 43, 72, 103
joyous, 66
judgement, 2, 76, 116
judgement biases, 2
justice, 83

K

kindliness, 54
kindness, 65
kisses, 56, 92, 97, 122
knight, 115
knowledge, 3, 29, 60

L

landscape, 79
laughing, 53

laughter, 78, 82
laundry, 117
leaden, 43, 72
learning, 46
liberation, 39
life, 2, 3, 7, 12, 13, 14, 15, 24, 25, 26, 28, 39, 45, 59, 61, 63, 65, 67, 68, 79, 80, 94, 113, 115, 116, 118, 120
lipstick, 59
lonely, 42, 94, 95, 118
loss, 2, 50, 86, 95
lost, 18, 50, 63, 86, 95, 122
love, 2, 11, 16, 17, 20, 21, 22, 25, 31, 33, 34, 35, 36, 37, 40, 41, 49, 50, 51, 53, 54, 56, 57, 63, 66, 69, 75, 77, 81, 82, 83, 84, 85, 86, 87, 89, 90, 91, 92, 93, 95, 98, 103, 115, 117, 122, 123, 124
luck, 11
luck-lustered, 116
luggage, 109
lust, 110

lying, 90

M

meaning, 2, 3, 23
medical, 29
memories, 25, 63
mercurial, 43, 72
mercy, 83
mind, 2, 42, 60, 92, 114, 121
misery, 108
mist, 63, 64, 107
monochrome, 120
mother, 74, 76, 114
motherhood, 75
mutual, 23, 66, 78, 84
myself, 31

N

naked, 113
nature, 1, 76, 118

noise, 48
nurture, 66, 118

O

obfuscate, 69
objective, 46, 68
obsessing, 53
odds, 60
odious, 112
oppression, 23
optimistic, 118
overload, 15, 28

P

partners, 19
passion, 66, 101
path, 43, 50, 72, 81, 86
peace, 51, 80, 82, 87, 95, 103, 113, 114, 118, 119, 121
perception, 105

perfection, 10
photo, 26
pillows, 97
poetic thoughts, 1
power, 100, 112
powerlessness, 113
practicality, 105
prescience, 9
pride, 48, 56, 112
progress, 60, 114
psycho-virginity, 68
puppetry, 34
purpose, 2, 19, 24, 25, 36, 46, 68, 124

Q

questions, 105

R

rapture, 101, 117

reactions, 48
realisation, 45, 67
reality, 120
rebel, 88
rebirth, 49
recognition, 47, 65
Recording, 26
regret, 17, 56
rejected, 21
rejection, 98
relationships, 5, 16, 17, 20, 23
reliving, 26
reminiscence, 95
resentment, 48, 62
resign, 22
resist, 52
respect, 34, 117
return, 25, 37, 46, 68, 103
reverse, 15, 28
ridicule, 106

S

safe, 35
safety, 34
sanctimonious, 112
sapphire, 84
science, 61
screaming, 108
sea, 76, 79, 84
secrets, 33, 122
security, 75
self, 25, 34, 35, 36, 62, 74, 75, 119, 121, 122
selfless, 56, 70, 100
Senryu, 1, 5, 8, 29
sensibility, 69
separation, 16
serenity, 51, 80, 87
servitude, 22
shadows, 66
sharing, 103
simplicity, 105

sincerity, 51, 87
singleton, 42
slip and fall, 81
smile, 54, 55, 61
smiling, 11, 55
solitude, 25, 95
Solomon's eye, 116
soul, 45, 46, 51, 54, 67, 68, 70, 87, 101
souls, 38, 123
special, 92
spirit, 61, 70
spiritual, 2
spirituality, 69
Spring, 57, 66, 97
stars, 38, 84
strife, 94
success, 39, 106
success, 11, 39
succinctness, 26
succour, 112
suitors, 99

sun and stars, 59
surrender, 118
syllable, 1, 7
symphonic, 76

T

tabula rasa, 46
tainted, 7
teaching, 47, 103
tears, 63, 119
tempting, 9
tender, 92, 97
tenderness, 100, 121
tension, 109
thankful, 43, 72
thinking slow, 7
thought, 51, 56, 68, 73, 87, 98
thoughts, 3, 7, 122
time, 2, 37, 41, 42, 81, 99, 100, 104, 105, 106, 109
togetherness, 104

training, 46
troubled, 60
trust, 34, 60, 61, 81, 90, 100, 121, 122
trusting, 36

U

unashamed, 100
unborn, 49
uncertainty, 33, 95, 121
unconditional, 70
undecided, 15, 28
understanding, 3, 26, 78, 122
unempowered, 112
unique, 21, 95
uniqueness, 45, 67
unite, 123, 124
unknown, 12, 14
unrequited, 42
unwilling, 16, 43, 72
usefulness, 62

V

vacuous souls, 89
vain, 89, 92
value, 8, 20, 103
vanity, 112
villain, 115
vulnerability, 33

W

waiting, 34, 35, 36
warmth, 64, 120
welfare, 74
wife, 94
wind, 76
wisdom, 8, 47
withdrawn, 21
worrying, 29
worth, 78, 89
worthy, 75, 83
wrong, 29, 92, 115

Y

yesterdays, 111

Z

zero, 13
zero Sum, 13

www.ingramcontent.com/pod-product-compliance
Lightning Source LLC
Chambersburg PA
CBHW072200070526
44585CB00015B/1228